How to Move on after a Breakup

*An Essential Guide
to Getting over a Relationship
and Moving on after a Breakup*

by Perina Lewes

Table of Contents

Introduction 1

Chapter 1: Handling the Breakup with CARE 7

Chapter 2: How to Give Yourself Space 15

Chapter 3: Coping with Your Emotions Appropriately 19

Chapter 4: Reviving Your Social Life 23

Chapter 5: How to Motivate Yourself to Keep Moving on . 27

Conclusion 31

Introduction

Human beings are social creatures by nature. We thrive on social interaction, and relationships play an important role in our lives. They affect us in many ways. For one, our relationships can determine our happiness and shape our character.

We get involved in different kinds of relationships with other people. We nurture relationships with our friends, family, and partners. All of them are important to us, but romantic relationships have quite a significant impact in our lives. Generally, we enter them with a perspective of the future. We invest a lot of our time, effort, and emotions into this kind of relationship in hopes of establishing our own families and sharing the rest of our lives with someone.

We also share a profound connection with our romantic partners. Although our friends and family know us up to a certain level, we tend to open up more of ourselves to our romantic partners. After all, if we are to spend the rest of our years with someone, they might as well know every little thing about us.

This is why it is difficult when romantic relationships end. Whatever the reason for the breakup is, and whether the decision is mutual or not, a breakup has the potential to turn our world upside down. Emotionally, it triggers painful feelings that, if not controlled, can lead us to indulge in self-destructive behavior and nervous breakdowns. A breakup can be so devastating that some do not even recover at all.

However, a breakup can also be the best thing that can happen to a person. With the right perspective, such a painful experience can be turned into a positive one. A breakup can be taken as a period of learning and self-discovery that can lead to personal development and even personal breakthroughs.

As you read this book, your perspective about breakups will be changed. This book will teach you how to get over a broken relationship and move on *the right way*. It does not guarantee that it will relieve you of all the hurt feelings that you might be suffering because of a breakup, but it assures to guide you as you step into the wonderful process of moving on.

© Copyright 2015 by Miafn LLC - All rights reserved.

This document is geared towards providing reliable information in regards to the topic and issue covered. The publication is sold with the idea that the publisher is not required to render accounting, officially permitted, or otherwise, qualified services. If advice is necessary, legal or professional, a practiced individual in the profession should be ordered.

- From a Declaration of Principles which was accepted and approved equally by a Committee of the American Bar Association and a Committee of Publishers and Associations.

In no way is it legal to reproduce, duplicate, or transmit any part of this document in either electronic means or in printed format. Recording of this publication is strictly prohibited and any storage of this document is not allowed unless with written permission from the publisher. All rights reserved.

The information provided herein is stated to be truthful and consistent, in that any liability, in terms of inattention or otherwise, by any usage or abuse of any policies, processes, or directions contained within is solely and completely the responsibility of the recipient reader. Under no circumstances will any legal responsibility or blame be held against the publisher for any reparation, damages, or monetary loss due to the information herein, either directly or indirectly.

Respective authors own all copyrights not held by the publisher.

The information herein is offered for informational purposes solely, and is universal as so. The presentation of the information is without contract or any type of guarantee assurance.

The trademarks that are used are without any consent, and the publication of the trademark is without permission or backing by the trademark owner. All trademarks and brands within this book are for clarifying purposes only and are the owned by the owners themselves, not affiliated with this document.

Chapter 1: Handling the Breakup with CARE

As kids, we were always advised to handle fragile things with care. A breakup is an extremely fragile thing. When handled recklessly, a breakup can bring sorrow and pain into our lives. That is why, like a breakable piece of precious glass, we should handle it with utmost care. Care, however in this book, represents four important things that we need to remember in handling a breakup:

Contemplate

Accept

Release and

Evaluate

The initial stage is often the most painful. The memories are still fresh and you replay them like an old film inside your head. The loneliness also scares you. It is something new and you haven't adjusted to it just yet. It is also in this stage that you are going to go through a mental warfare. A thousand thoughts, questions and what ifs are racing inside your head and you can't seem to get a grip of yourself. You try to rest but you can't. You try to eat but you can't either.

This situation leads to a feeling of helplessness. However, do not be discouraged. Breakups are only excruciating in the beginning but if you handle it with CARE, you will feel the pain gradually subside.

Contemplate on your breakup

This first step sounds simple but it is difficult to do. Why should you purposely think of something that you are trying to forget? Let us be realistic. We can forget little things like our car keys and appointments but we will never forget relationships. We can only either accept them or deny them and push them to the back of our heads. The mind is not like a computer hard drive. We cannot delete memories even if we want to, so forgetting a breakup is basically impossible.

Acceptance leads to moving on but it does not come right away. There are some who are mature enough to accept a breakup, especially if it is a mutual decision. Nonetheless, the majority of people who are fresh out of a breakup are still in denial. If you find yourself in such a situation, do not feel hopeless. Acceptance is possible if you are willing to do the first step: **contemplate on your breakup**.

Contemplating on your breakup is clearing your mind of all the strong emotions that you are feeling. A good way to do so is to meditate before you start thinking. There are many forms of meditation depending on your preferences. Whether you like to meditate with the use of music or to meditate with the help of nature, there are many sources both online and offline that you can access to find the perfect form of meditation that will suit you. When you and your thoughts are finally relaxed, you can proceed with the thinking process.

Think of the reason why you broke up. Even if you believe that your relationship ended for no good reason, there certainly was one, or there might have been more than one. Healthily contemplating will open your eyes to the truth that you are turning a blind eye to. It puts into perspective that your relationship wasn't really working out and that even if you didn't breakup, you were bound to fall apart sooner or later. It makes you discover the reality of what was really going on and when you finally see the truth, you move on to the next step which is acceptance.

Accept what has come to pass

Acceptance is a vital part of getting over a broken relationship. Without acceptance, you are stuck in denial and unable to move on. If you are able to accept your breakup whole heartedly, it becomes a freeing process that releases you from all the pain and sorrow.

Where does acceptance start? It starts in your mind. To achieve acceptance, we must cultivate certain thoughts in our heads. It does not come instantly either. Acceptance comes with constant reminders and a genuine change in our mindset.

To accept your breakup, you must educate your mind to understanding that relationships are learning experiences. Certain people come into our lives to help us become the strong and mature person that we are meant to be. However, some of these people will not stay in our lives. Some of them leave, whether they be a friend or a special someone. That is just how life works. It doesn't teach its lessons in classrooms. Its lessons come in the form of other people, and often in the form of romantic partners. You have to let this fact of life sink in.

You also have to understand that it takes two people for a relationship to work. Even if you are committed to loving the other person with every bit of your heart and soul, if the other is not, your relationship is surely bound to fail. There is no point in forcing someone to get back together when it is only you who is dedicated to making it work. Remember, relationships are not a one-way street. No matter how much the other person means to you, you have to use your head and be rational. Accept that it is over.

<u>Release the past</u>

Now that you have learned to accept your breakup, the next step is to release the past. Imagine yourself holding on to something with both hands. In order to hold on to something new, you have to let go of what you currently have. You can't possibly hold the two things at the same time. You will end up dropping and breaking them both.

The same is true in a breakup. In order to hold on to something new, which is the future, you have to let go of what you are holding on to, which is the past. It is virtually impossible to hold them both together. So you have to let go of one. Now that you have learned to accept that it is no use holding on to the past, we already know which one to let go of.

There are various ways to release the past. Releasing our emotions is one effective way. Cry it out. Scream if you have to. However, make sure that you are expressing yourself healthily. Do not scream or lash out at other people. This is a process that you need to do by yourself.

Another effective method to release your emotions is through materializing the process. In an episode of Desperate Housewives, Gabrielle Solis (played by famous actress Eva Longoria) was suffering from depression due to a miscarriage. In order to release the emotional burden, her husband Carlos asked a friend to help her let go of her emotions through a balloon. The friend took her to an open field where Gabrielle walked to the center and released the balloon as a symbol of her releasing her pain. This is not just simply a melodramatic gesture. This method is actually supported by psychology.

According to several scientific studies, if we materialize our pain, it becomes easier to let go. That is why making use of objects such as a balloon can prove useful in releasing our emotions. Writing is also one way of materializing our pain. We translate our emotions into words, and the writing process becomes a freeing experience.

It also helps to "physically" release the past by ridding ourselves of things that remind us of it. Whether it is an anniversary gift from your former lover or the keepsake ticket from your first movie together, it significantly helps to throw or give it away. Such an action may seem a bit harsh, but freeing yourself of reminders of the past will help you to move on.

Evaluate your present self

Before putting yourself out there again, it is best to evaluate yourself. What were your weaknesses throughout the relationship? How have you grown and changed since? What areas of yourself as a partner do you need to improve on? Asking yourself these questions will help you avoid making the same mistakes in the future. If you open yourself to new relationships without working on your flaws or weaknesses first, you will end up with another broken relationship. You do not need another breakup to deal with.

Chapter 2: How to Give Yourself Space

Even if you and your ex have agreed to stay friends despite your breakup, you have to break away completely from him. This is not a way of expressing your anger and resentment. Instead, giving yourself space is giving yourself time: time to focus on building yourself up again.

Relationships have a way of draining our time and energy, so that during a breakup, you realize that you have spent months or years taking care of another person. You might also realize that in that span of time, you have spent too little time on yourself.

You deserve some "me-time." After devoting a significant amount of your time and energy on another person, it is now time to give yourself some rest. Enroll yourself at a fitness club. Take on a new hobby. Spend quality time with your friends. Basically, just do whatever you have always wanted to do. Being free from the responsibilities that come with being in a relationship now gives you time to tick off items in your bucket list.

One way of giving yourself space is to cut all communication between you and your ex. When you have so many questions and thoughts brewing inside your head, it is tempting to contact your former lover in an attempt to "straighten" things out. You can prevent yourself from committing this grave mistake by deleting all his contact information. Although it isn't necessarily a permanent measure, it is needed while you undergo the moving on process. Make sure that you cut all ties with your ex on your phone, social media, e-mail, instant messengers and other forms of communication.

As much as you love his friends and family members, you must avoid seeing and talking to them too. Again, this isn't a permanent measure. You can always resume your friendship with them in time. If they ask why you are avoiding them, just politely explain why. They will understand your decision.

Giving yourself space does not only involve cutting ties with your ex. It also involves limiting your social interaction with other people including your friends. Hanging out with them might help you escape the feelings that you are dealing with and surely, being your good friends, they will be happy to help you cope with your breakup. It will feel nice having people care for you but there is a right time for that later after you have already fully recovered. For now, it is best to spend some time alone so your thoughts will remain uninterrupted. Take this time to listen to yourself.

Being alone will be difficult. Fresh from a breakup, you will feel desperate and needy. You will seek the company of other people to fill up the gaping hole inside you. This is not the healthy way to deal with a breakup. You should be responsible for building yourself up, and not depend on other people. Do not be scared of being alone. It will bring you face to face with the pain and sorrow but there is no other way to deal with them but to fight them head on. If you run away from them, they will eventually catch up, but if you face them without fear, you will be able to deal with them once and for all.

Do not let people fool you into thinking that you cannot deal with a breakup all by yourself. Always bear in mind that you are strong enough and that you should never allow yourself to fall into the habit of being dependent on other people. If you put your stability in the hands of others, what happens if they leave your life? You get torn in pieces again. Do not make that mistake. Likewise, being able to survive a breakup on your own will allow you to love yourself. You will emerge stronger, braver and with a healthy amount of self-respect. You will learn to be your own best friend and you will learn to approach your future relationships with a wiser perspective.

Chapter 3: Coping with Your Emotions Appropriately

Emotions are hard to control. They have the potential to overwhelm us and take over our thoughts and actions. This is why in some breakups, people engage themselves in self-destructive behavior. They use substances like alcohol to escape from the emotions that are plaguing them. Although they are able to forget their pain momentarily, it eventually finds a way to creep back in, especially when they are already beginning to sober up.

Getting involved in rebound relationships is also an unhealthy way to cope with your emotions. Using another person to relieve yourself of pain is a selfish thing to do. It is harmful to your character and will only get you in conflict with the party involved. Do not hurt other people just because you are in pain. Put yourself in their shoes. Surely you do not want to be in a relationship where you are only being used by an emotionally unstable person. You, of all people, should know what it is like to have your heart broken. Do not cause other people to experience the same burden.

Sadly, there are yet others who use seriously harmful ways to deal with the pain. There are some people who physically hurt themselves while some attempt or commit suicide. We are not condemning them for the choice that they have made, but we should be aware of the danger and avoid going down that path ourselves. No matter how unbearable your emotions get, do not allow them to drive you to destroying or killing yourself. Always remember that there is hope and that what you are going through is just a temporary phase. Sooner or later, you will be able to break from the chains of the past and claim the many wonderful things that await you in the future. Even if you think this is the end, it certainly is not. Do not think of giving up the fight.

There are many ways to cope with your emotions appropriately. These ways will help you acquire a new skill, meet new people and improve yourself, in general. One literally healthy way that you can deal with the pain is through engaging yourself in physical activities. According to science, an ample amount of exercise generates happy hormones which make you feel better. Likewise, being involved in a physical activity also significantly contributes to your character formation and self-confidence. It allows you to develop discipline and patience, while protecting and improving your overall health. Involving yourself in a competitive sport is also a great option. When you are training for a competition, you are giving yourself a goal to achieve. This will give you the drive and direction that you lack after a breakup leaves you feeling inadequate, helpless and seemingly hopeless.

Others also find involvement in religious activities to be a healthy and effective way to cope with their emotions. Just as other people with other problems recover with divine intervention, you can too, if you choose to.

You can also consider taking on hobbies that you have neglected in the past. If you have a book in mind that you have always wanted to read, now is the right time to do it. If you have missed your dancing classes for dates with your former partner, now is also the right moment to wear your dancing shoes again. Cope with your emotions appropriately, by becoming involved in wholesome activities!

Chapter 4: Reviving Your Social Life

Now that you are ready, it is about time that you put yourself out there. This is not only for you to find a new partner but also for you to rekindle ties that you paid little attention to while you were still in a relationship.

When we are in a relationship, we have to make certain sacrifices. This often includes spending less time with our family and friends. Because of our high hopes of a future with our partner, we invest most of our time working on our relationship that we tend to neglect the other people in our lives. Although some people are able to manage this quite well, we have to admit that we cannot balance our time without making compromises. For example, if we want to spend an equal amount of time with our friends, family and partner, we have to sacrifice our "me time." However, do not take this negatively. This is practically the essence of being in a relationship. When we love someone, we should be able to make certain sacrifices.

Recovering from a breakup is also the best time to recover these relationships that we have sacrificed. We can start off with the people who are closest to us, our family. Spend more time with them and allow the warmth of home to comfort you during your dark times. Our family loves us unconditionally and if we are feeling lonely, there is no better way to feel loved than to go home and feel the great love of our relatives embrace us. Your family loves you and they will be supportive in what you are going through. Open up your heart and let them help you in the healing process.

This is also a great time to reconnect with friends. Even though you are not related by blood, they care for you as well. Get in touch with friends who you weren't able to contact over the past months or years. Have a friendly outing together and enjoy it just like the old times. You will be surprised at how fast and easy you will be able to cope with your breakup if you open yourself up to your friends again.

If you feel that you are ready, open yourself up to meeting new people. It will feel uncomfortable at first, especially if you just came out of a long-term relationship. It will feel as though you don't know how to approach people anymore. Just ***be you***. Be confident. Breakups have a way of killing your self-esteem, but don't let it anchor you down. You have an amazing personality so let it show. Make friends with someone new. Tell them about yourself, your interests, and just let your light shine through. One tip that you should never forget, though: as much as possible, refrain from mentioning your breakup. In order to build new bridges, you have to burn the old ones. There's no use repeating the story of your split and letting it define you. You would want people to know you for who you truly are and not for your breakup.

Dating opportunities will be presented to you as you make friends with new people. Taking them on is ultimately up to you and your evaluation of yourself. If you feel like you are ready to date other people, do so with caution. Do not rush into committing yourself to another romantic relationship. Take it slow and take the time to build a strong friendship with the other person first. On the other hand, if you feel that you are not ready yet, do not force yourself. There is no law imposed on you, forcing you to date again right after the breakup. For some, it takes a longer time to be ready for a relationship once again, so do not pressure yourself. Date at your own pace.

Chapter 5: How to Motivate Yourself to Keep Moving on

In this phase of your life, you are your own best friend. There will be a lot of people who will motivate and support you, but do you know where the strongest form of motivation comes from? It comes from within you. You should learn how to constantly motivate yourself because at the end of the day, when everyone is busy with their own lives, you will be left with nobody but your own self.

There are many ways that you can motivate yourself that do not involve complicated psychological processes to condition your mind positively. A simple way is to make use of daily reminders to keep yourself focused on moving on. With the advent of technology, you can make use of digital reminders on your mobile phone, computers or tablets. There are numerous mobile applications that can help in your recovery like applications that give you a new inspirational quote daily.

Motivational books and other forms of literature are also available on the market. Get one and try to read it every day so that you will be reminded to stay on track. Likewise, reading will enable you to understand that you are not alone in your journey. There are also other people who have been where you are at this point of your life and yet, they were able to successfully recover and build happier relationships in the end.

If you are the creative type, you can make a painting, a poster or other forms of art that you can display in your bedroom or on your office table. Whenever you are feeling down, instead of wallowing in pain and sorrow once again, just look at the reminder that you have made. This idea is so simple that you might think that it is trivial. However, there will come a time that you will be grateful for the little reminders that you have set for yourself.

Motivation involves maintaining positive thoughts and a matching positive attitude. It will be a challenge to be cheerful and optimistic in the face of pain but if you want to move on, you have to do your best to motivate yourself. Nobody is going to do the job for you. Your family and friends can only go so far. If you are not willing to help yourself, you will be stuck in this phase for a very long time. You don't want that to happen. You don't want to regret missing out on the amazing future that awaits you.

Conclusion

This is not the end for you. Imagine your life as a thick book with each significant event and person in your life taking up a particular chapter. The relationship that you had is just one of the many chapters that comprise the story of your life. It is only a small part, and not the end of your book, so do not give up and close your book just yet. Even if it feels as though this is already the last chapter of your life, you are wrong. There are still many chapters for you to write, but only if you choose to recover.

Do not choose the pain. Choose to heal. Ultimately, how long you will stay in this phase is up to you. If you choose to get stuck in sorrow and pain, then that is what will happen. However, if you follow the different lessons being taught in this book and strive to turn your painful experience into a learning one, you will come out of this breakup as a stronger and happier person.

Never lose hope. Compare yourself to a diamond that is being refined to perfection. In order for a diamond to truly shine, it has to go through extreme heat. You are a diamond and you have a brilliant shine waiting to be revealed. All this pain and disappointment are your refiner's fire that will shape you into perfection. Do not allow yourself to melt as you go through the heat. Fight it, and shine brighter than ever.

Finally, I'd like to thank you for purchasing this book! If you found it helpful, I'd greatly appreciate it if you'd take a moment to leave a review on Amazon. Thank you!

Made in the USA
Las Vegas, NV
14 December 2023